Multicultural Activities for the Public Speaking Classroom

Marlene C. Cohen
Susan L. Richardson
Tony D. Hawkins
Prince George's Community College

HOUGHTON MIFFLIN COMPANY   BOSTON   NEW YORK

Sponsoring Editor: George Hoffman
Editorial Assistant/Editorial: Kara Maltzahn
Editorial Assistant/Editorial Production: Rebecca Bennett
Associate Production Coordinator: Deborah Frydman
Senior Manufacturing Coordinator: Marie Barnes

Printed in the U.S.A.

ISBN: 0-395-83994-7
6789-MD-00 99 98 97

Multicultural Activities for the Public Speaking Classroom

Introduction

We began the project of creating multicultural exercises for introductory speech communication classes because we felt the intercultural dimensions of communication are too important to be left as elective study. Our society is becoming more diverse and the workplace already consists of people from a variety of backgrounds and cultures. To be successful in the workplace and in our personal relationships, it is essential to communicate effectively with a wide variety of people.

More than most classes, your speech communication class is a good place for you to become more aware of multicultural issues. You will learn how to adapt to your listeners. You will become more aware of yourself as a communicator and become more aware of the ways in which you are similar to and different from classmates in values, attitudes, language use, and nonverbal communication.

We hope your class will be a comfortable place to address the vital topics of race, ethnicity, class, gender, sexual orientation, disabilities, etc., in our society. Along with developing an understanding and respect for diversity, you will also be practicing many communication skills that can improve your ability to be flexible in your communication. Hopefully you will build a repertoire of ways of responding and develop sensitivity to making the appropriate communication choices at the appropriate times.

The terms below should help you with the multicultural approach you will be taking in this class.

TERMS TO KNOW

Culture—the learned product of group experience,[1] including artifacts, concepts such as values and belief systems, and behaviors.[2] In the United States people belong to cultures composed of various religious, economic, ethnic, age, gender, sexual preference, and racial groups.[3]

Diversity—"differences among people or peoples reflected in a variety of forms, such as race, culture, perspective, talent, interest, age, or religion."[4]

[1]National MultiCultural Institute, *Training of Trainers: Developing Cultural Diversity Programs for the Workplace,* (Washington, D.C.: National MultiCultural Institute, 1993).

[2]Richard E. Porter and Larry A. Samovar, "An Introduction to Intercultural Communication," in *Intercultural Communication: A Reader*, 7th ed., eds. Larry A. Samavor and Richard E. Porter (Belmont, CA: Wadsworth Publishing Company, 1994), p. 11.

[3]Larry A. Samovar and Richard E. Porter, *Intercultural Communication: A Reader*, 7th ed. (Belmont, CA: Wadsworth Publishing Company, 1994), p. 125.

[4]National MultiCultural Institute, *Training of Trainers: Developing Cultural Diversity Programs for the Workplace*, (Washington, D.C.: National MultiCultural Institute, 1993).

Ethnocentrism—"the tendency to interpret and evaluate others' behavior using our own standards." This leads to viewing the in-group's ways of doing things as natural and thus superior to other groups' ways.[5]

Intercultural communication—any communication situation in which the message to be understood "is produced by a member of one culture for consumption by a member of another culture."[6]

ACKNOWLEDGMENTS

The original activity manual would not have been possible without the support of Prince George's Community College and Title III, United States Department of Education. We are grateful for that opportunity. We also thank Michael Kidwell for his computer expertise and Elliott Oppenheim, Meaghan Doyle, Brendan Doyle, and Alexander Kidwell for their patience.

Marlene C. Cohen
Susan L. Richardson
Tony D. Hawkins

[5]William B. Gudykunst, *Bridging Differences: Effective Intergroup Communication*, 2nd ed. (Thousand Oaks, CA: Sage Publications, Inc., 1994), p. 78.

[6]Porter and Samovar, *Intercultural Communication: A Reader*, p. 19.

Achieving Success in Public Speaking Class

CHAPTER 1: INTRODUCTORY ACTIVITIES

Objectives

- To orient yourself to what *strong* students do.

- To determine important student behaviors which you would like to improve.

Steps

1. Read the "Action Rules for Successful Students" list on the following page.

2. In writing, sign on to the first three rules and write in your own words your commitment to try to do well.

3. Then put into writing the other items on the list that you wish to accomplish this semester to succeed in this class.

4. Finally put into writing what your instructor can do to help you achieve your goals. Tell him/her of anything going on in your life that might get in the way of your success this semester.

*INSTRUCTOR: See Exercise Notes for this exercise in the back of the book.

Action Rules for Successful Students

Creators choose their own rules. Circle all of the action rules below that you commit yourself to following this semester to reach your goals. *Each commitment is a promise to yourself*; no one else will see your commitments unless you show them. Don't lie to yourself! CREATE AND FOLLOW YOUR OWN RULES!

1.   Attend every class from beginning to end.
2.   Do my best work on assignments and hand them in on time.
3.   Respect and support my classmates and teachers in achieving their dreams.
4.   Write down my long- and short-term goals.
5.   Review my goals often.
6.   Plan my weekly written schedule, including sufficient time to study.
7.   Take good notes in every class.
8.   Review my notes often.
9.   Make appointments to talk with my instructors about anything that confuses me.
10.   Seek out and use a tutor.
11.   Nurture myself: get proper rest, eat well, exercise regularly.
12.   Study and learn from the written feedback I get from instructors on my assignments.
13.   Associate with winners and positive people.
14.   Follow directions carefully.
15.   Use the library.
16.   Avoid drugs and excessive use of alcohol.
17.   Bring course tools (books, notebooks, pens, etc.) to every class.
18.   Do assignments early.
19.   Find a good study place and study there often.
20.   Strive for excellence; do more than just enough to get by.
21.   Laugh and have fun.
22.   Write a visualization of my goals; read it often.
23.   Participate, volunteer, and get involved in class.
24.   Listen carefully.
25.   Enjoy my classes.
26.   Post our course affirmations at home and say them daily.
27.   Compete with myself to do better than last time.
28.   Give myself frequent small rewards for daily successes.
29.   Talk positively to myself.
30.   Say a prayer.
31.   Talk in class when appropriate; otherwise, focus on the speaker.

32. Request assistance from family and friends when needed.

33. Join or create a study group.

34. Take frequent breaks while studying.

35. Read difficult assignments twice or even three times.

36. Create possible test questions to study from.

37. Go to the appropriate lab (science, reading, writing, math, computer, etc.)

38. Complete my college assignments before socializing.

39. Look at myself in the mirror every day and say, "You are a master student."

40. Remind myself daily that I am capable, lovable, and worthy of a great life.

Source: From Skip Downing, *On Course: Strategies for Creating Success in College and in Life*. Copyright © 1996 by Houghton Mifflin Company. Adapted with permission.

East-West Assumptions

CHAPTER 1: INTRODUCTORY ACTIVITIES

Objectives

- To identify the Western values with which we generally operate.

- To identify contrasting Eastern values, alternatives to many of our common values.

- To recognize how differences in values can result in conflicting points of view and behaviors.

Steps

1. Write a paragraph or two describing a specific conflict situation you have experienced with a person or people from a cultural background different from yours, being Eastern or Western. *Eastern* as used here includes Asian and other indigenous cultures, such as Native American Indian cultures. *Western* refers to nations whose systems of law and of reasoning stem from Greek and Judeo-Christian tradition. Of course, all such categorizing is generalization that cannot be applied as absolute to all situations or people.

2. Use information from the following list of assumptions and values. What values and behaviors distinguish the perspectives of the person or people involved in your situation? Why might you differ in your opinions or expectations?

3. Discuss how the differing values can be understood, modified, or directed to reconcile the conflict toward greater harmony or productivity.

*INSTRUCTOR: See Exercise Notes for this exercise in the back of the book.

Summary of Underlying Assumptions and Values

WESTERN	EASTERN
***Western* refers to nations whose origins of law and of reasoning stem from Greek and Judeo-Christian tradition.**	**_Eastern_ as used here includes Asian and other indigenous cultures, such as Native American Indian cultures.**
Universe is created and controlled by divine power.	Universe unfolds itself, not caused by outside power.
Universe is a lifeless mass.	Universe is one vast living organism, continually changing and impermanent.
Universe separates the knowing human from things to know.	Universe is one vast living organism of many interrelated forces and parts; humans are a part of life force.
Thinking leads to clear and distinct ideas in categories.	Things are known holistically, not by analysis; thinking leads to imprecise statements.
Knowledge leads to awareness of specific facts.	Purpose of knowledge is to see unity of all things.
Knowledge comes from scientific method and analytical logic.	Knowledge comes from intuition.
Growth can lead to social change.	Growth can lead to oneness with the universe.
Time is moving from past toward future; humans synchronize their time with clocks and machines.	Time is a continuous wheel; humans synchronize their time with nature.
Individual needs may come before group.	Group conformity is necessary for unity.
Communication is direct and verbal.	Communication is indirect and often silent; understanding is often grasped by observation.

Adapted from Young Yun Kim, "Intercultural Personhood: An Integration of Eastern and Western Perspectives," in *Intercultural Communication : A Reader*, 7th ed., eds. Larry A. Samovar and Richard E. Porter (Belmont, CA: Wadsworth Publishing Company, 1994), pp. 415–425.

The Culture Iceberg

CHAPTER 1: INTRODUCTORY ACTIVITIES

Objectives

- To discuss elements of individual culture.

- To define "culture."

- To discuss how membership in a culture affects your perceptions of others and behaviors toward others.

Steps

1. Consider the following items and write your responses to each on paper:
   a. What groups are you a member of?
   b. Identify an important group for your self-identity: gender, class, race, religion, sexual preference, geography, etc.
   c. What have you observed other members of your group doing?
   d. Has your group ever discriminated against others?

2. Meet in small groups to discuss your answers.

3. Share with the full class group the similarities, differences, and trends your group discovered. Share observations and/or realizations.

4. Look at the "Culture Iceberg" model on the following page.

5. Read the following:
   A person's race, gender, or physical disability may be his or her most obvious characteristic, but region of the country or religious affiliation may be the most important characteristic to him or her. We can't judge others' group memberships by appearance.

   As with an iceberg, only one-tenth of who people are culturally is visible to others. It is what is below the surface that explains cultural behaviors. For an example, select one or two issues from the iceberg list that help to explain that some of your own behaviors are based on your own culture. For example:
   female gender—preference for cooperation, not competition
   Midwestern work ethic—incentives to work, work hard, do the best you can, etc.

6. Discuss how each of us chooses how to self-identify from among our many cultures.

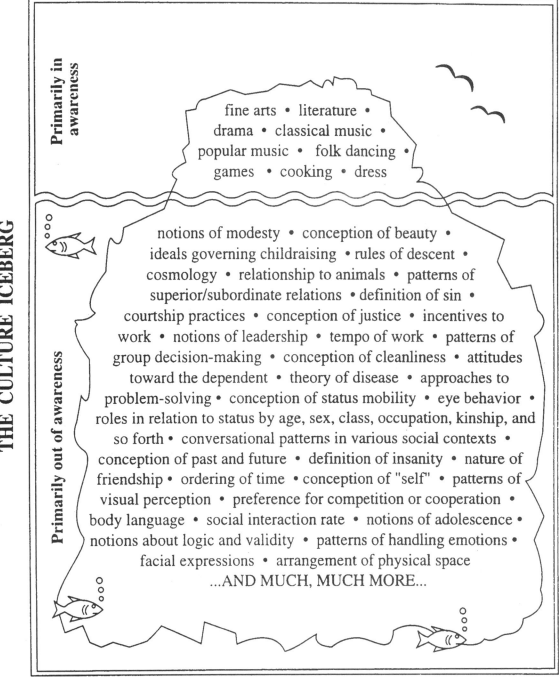

THE CULTURE ICEBERG

Primarily in awareness

fine arts • literature • drama • classical music • popular music • folk dancing • games • cooking • dress

Primarily out of awareness

notions of modesty • conception of beauty • ideals governing childraising • rules of descent • cosmology • relationship to animals • patterns of superior/subordinate relations • definition of sin • courtship practices • conception of justice • incentives to work • notions of leadership • tempo of work • patterns of group decision-making • conception of cleanliness • attitudes toward the dependent • theory of disease • approaches to problem-solving • conception of status mobility • eye behavior • roles in relation to status by age, sex, class, occupation, kinship, and so forth • conversational patterns in various social contexts • conception of past and future • definition of insanity • nature of friendship • ordering of time • conception of "self" • patterns of visual perception • preference for competition or cooperation • body language • social interaction rate • notions of adolescence • notions about logic and validity • patterns of handling emotions • facial expressions • arrangement of physical space ...AND MUCH, MUCH MORE...

Just as nine-tenths of an iceberg is out of sight (below the water line), so is nine-tenths of culture out of conscious awareness. The out-of-awareness part of culture has been termed "deep culture."

Source: AFS American Field Service, *AFS Student Yearbook and the Arrival Orientation*, (New York: AFS American Field Service), p. 71. Reprinted by permission of AFS American Field Service Intercultural Programs / USA.

Audience Survey

CHAPTER 2: AUDIENCE ANALYSIS

Objectives

- To create your own audience surveys.

- To develop objective questions, to tabulate results, to analyze results, and to adapt your speeches to your class audience.

Steps

1. Select a topic for a persuasive speech assignment.

2. Read sample survey questions.

3. Design an audience survey based on your speech topic.

4. When assigned, bring to class enough copies of your survey to hand out to everyone (including the instructor).

5. Tabulate your results.

6. Write two paragraphs indicating what you have learned from the class survey that will help you organize and present your persuasive speech. Answer these questions:

   a. What did you learn about this particular audience?
   b. How will you adapt to this audience in your speech?

*INSTRUCTOR: See Exercise Notes for this exercise in the back of the book.

Sample Survey

Sample Demographic Questions

1. Age _____

2. Sex: Male _____   Female _____

3. Relationship status:

   Married _____   Single _____   Widowed _____

   Divorced _____   Engaged _____

4. Number of children (if any) _____   Ages _____

5. Race or ethnic background _____

6. Religion _____

7. Year in college _____

8. Major _____

9. Organizations to which you belong

   _____

   _____

10. Jobs you have held_____

    _____

Sample Attitude Questions

Open-ended Questions

What do you think about homosexuality in America today?

Forced Choice

Is homosexuality a problem in America today? (Circle one)

YES   NO

Rate the concept on a continuum:

HOMOSEXUALITY IS A SERIOUS PROBLEM.

_____	_____	_____	_____	_____
strongly agree	agree	neutral	disagree	strongly disagree

Semantic Differential

HOMOSEXUALITY

Good ____ ____ ____ ____ ____ ____ ____ Bad

   1   2   3   4   5   6   7

Rank Order

Rank 1 through 5, where 1 equals the area of most concern to you, 5 equals the area of least concern to you.

_____ homelessness

_____ homosexuality

_____ AIDS

_____ gambling

_____ prostitution

Multiple Choice

Be sure to indicate whether to "check one" or "check all that apply."

If a very good friend of yours confided to you for the first
time that he or she is gay, what would you do?

_____ 1.   I would not associate with that friend again.

_____ 2.   I would listen carefully, but probably wouldn't say much.

_____ 3.   I would try to be supportive and tell my friend that his or her being gay does not
make a difference to me.

_____ 4.   I would refer my friend to a counselor so he or she could get help.

_____ 5.   I would try to get him or her to see this decision as an error in judgment and try
to get him or her to change.

Hints

The wording should be clear, complete, unbiased.
Give the full range of choices.
Give your survey to a few friends to test it before making your copies and distributing them
to your class.
The instructions must be clear.
Don't ask for names; give people privacy to answer honestly.

What Does My Audience Believe?

CHAPTER 2: AUDIENCE ANALYSIS

Objectives

- To acquaint you with your classroom audience's attitudes.

- To help you use this information on audience attitudes to select a speech topic and decide on an approach to presenting it.

Steps

1. Divide the classroom in half with tape, or a line dividing the chalkboard in half.

2. Designate one side of the room the "agree" side, the other side of the room the "disagree" side.

3. Everyone stand. Read the statements listed below one at a time. In response, all class members should vote with their feet. You must either agree or disagree with a statement. Walk to one side of the room as a public statement of belief.

4. Keep track of the overall class votes. You may want to put the voting topics on the board and tally votes each time. Thus if the class takes a stand on "Many students have experienced discrimination," you count how many agreed and how many disagreed with the statement.

5. At the completion of the exercise, some useful discussion questions would be as follows:

   Looking at the results of all of our votes, what generalizations could be made about this audience?
   What implications are there for topic selection and audience adaptation?

6. Examples of belief statements are as follows:
   Abortion is wrong.
   Many whites experience reverse discrimination.
   Anyone in the United States can make it if he or she works hard.
   People with disabilities should be mainstreamed into all aspects of American life.
   The death penalty is wrong.
   The African-American male is endangered.
   Same-sex unions (marriages) should be allowed.
   Free speech should be allowed on college campuses.
   AIDS is a worldwide health problem.
   Health care should be available to all Americans.
   College freshmen are poorly prepared for college success.

The United States is obligated to support our new immigrants.
The value placed on human life has diminished.
Women have made great strides in breaking the glass ceiling.
The United States has an obligation to attend to the health and educational needs of illegal immigrants.
Democracy is the best form of government.
Men have difficulty expressing their feelings.
Interracial adoptions are good for everyone.
Rap music denigrates women.

Feel free to choose from this list and add others of your own.

Adapting Your Speech Topic

CHAPTER 2: AUDIENCE ANALYSIS

Objectives

- To learn how speech topics may be altered to address the cultural climate of audiences.

- To gain assistance in the development of central ideas.

Steps

1. Imagine you are preparing to speak on the selected topics to the audiences described in the Audience-Adaptation Exercise.

2. Write central ideas for each topic and audience.

3. Report your central ideas to the class or submit written versions for evaluation.

Audience-Adaptation Exercise

Topic 1: Valuing Diversity

Audience A: A group of workers from the municipal parks commission: supervisors, recreation center managers, and police officers. 45% African-American, 40% white, 15% Hispanic-American; 70% males, 30% females.

Audience B: 25 members of a college fraternity attending as a component of their pledge education program. They assume that much of what they will learn during this session may be of little value to them once they are initiated. The group is racially balanced and between the ages of 18 and 22.

Topic 2: Working in an AIDS Hospice

Audience A: Members of your college or university student governance organization responsible for allocating funds to campus clubs. Their characteristics are those of your own college or university.

Audience B: Parents whose civic organization is looking for a charitable beneficiary for their annual fundraising drive. Their children (ages 8–14) have held car washes, summer carnivals, and bake sales in order to raise money for this year's recipient.

Analyzing Audiences from Different Cultures

CHAPTER 2: AUDIENCE ANALYSIS

Objectives

- To learn about high and low context cultures and monochronic and polychronic people.

- To analyze how to share information with mixed audiences.

Steps

1. Read the following page on high-low/monochronic-polychronic concepts.

2. Discuss the concepts, defining and illustrating the terms listed above with specific examples.

   Some useful topics to discuss would be the following:

   In low context cultures people prefer to get a great deal of information, detailed hand-outs, and clearly organized information. The speaker should stay within planned topics. Often audiences are very blunt about questions and consider it the speaker's responsibility to make ideas clear. His or her academic credentials are important.

   In high context cultures speakers provide less information, assuming the audience knows the subject. They can discuss a variety of topics with credible information. Audiences might like handouts that are more pictorial and less direct than ones with specific data. It is the responsibility of the listener to understand the information. Credibility in high context cultures is based more on the status of the organization the speaker represents than on the speaker.

   High context cultures: Asians, Arabs, Russians

   Low context cultures: Americans, Australians, Scandinavians, Germans, Swiss

   Middle context cultures: Africans, Southern Europeans, South Americans

3. Divide into small groups and read the following "Case Study." Decide as a group what you would do to adapt to a mixed audience.

4. A student from each group should report to the class the group's recommendations for approaching this particular audience.

High-Low/Monochronic-Polychronic Concepts

HIGH CONTEXT CULTURES

(Most information understood from the physical context or is internalized in the person.)

Nonverbal messages are important.
Environment is important.
Expect communicators to understand unarticulated feelings, subtle gestures.
Verbal codes less important (may be perceived as nondisclosive, sneaky, mysterious).
Information flows freely.
Extensive information networks exist.
Interruptions are accepted.
Schedules are not very important.

LOW CONTEXT CULTURES

(Most information is provided in specific and explicit language.)

Nonverbal messages and environment are less important.

Verbal codes more important (may be perceived as excessively talkative, redundant).
Specific information from an authority is preferred.
Detailed information is preferred.
Sophisticated information networks are lacking.
Information is organized and classified.
Information is provided if needed.
Information is power.

POLYCHRONIC PEOPLE

Are easily interrupted.
Are high context, usually will have information.
Value commitments.
Are relationship oriented.
Are flexible in planning.
Prefer to do several tasks at once.

MONOCHRONIC PEOPLE

Prefer to do one thing at a time.
Are low context, need information.
Take deadlines and schedules seriously.
Would try not to disturb conversations.
Concentrate on the job to be done.
Like to stick to the plan.

Sources:
Peter Andersen, "Explaining Intercultural Differences in Nonverbal Communication," in *Intercultural Communication: A Reader*, 7th ed., eds. Larry A. Samovar and Richard E. Porter. (Belmont, CA: Wadsworth Publishing Company, 1994), pp. 229–239.

Rebecca Reisner, "How Different Cultures Learn," *Meeting News*, 17 (June 1993), pp. 30–32.

Case Study

You work in upper-level management in a large multinational corporation. Your largest production plants are located in the United States (Omaha) and in Japan (Tokyo). The company is holding a joint meeting of mid-level and higher production managers because soon the plants in both the United States and Japan will be instituting a new production system. You are charged with the responsibility of explaining the primary changes in production that will be taking place at the plants.

A. Assume there are about 50 people in your audience. The audience is about half Japanese and half American. Applying what you have been discussing about high-low/monochronic-polychronic cultures, how would you approach this audience?

What would be important about the physical environment?
What kind of visuals would you use?
What would you assume the audience already knows?
What materials might you provide?
What style of presentation would you use?
Would you allow questions during the presentation?
What aspects of delivery would be important to you?

B. Answer the questions above, assuming

1. a predominantly American audience.

2. a predominantly Japanese audience.

The Tour

CHAPTER 2: AUDIENCE ANALYSIS

Objectives

- To emphasize the importance of careful audience analysis.

- To identify culture-specific behavior of daily exchanges on your campus.

- To develop accuracy in identifying the steps in the performance of a process.

Steps

1. Select a culture-specific behavior typically demonstrated on your campus — i.e., a greeting behavior, particular artifacts which are frequently on display (such as the school mascot), a frequent argument made by faculty members, or the rules for proper cafeteria etiquette.

2. Define on paper an audience of strangers from another country, planet, or metaphysical plane.

3. Write a 3 to 4 minute informative speech for this audience, detailing how a person would perform this function properly. Be sure that your speech includes the importance and history associated with this ceremony, ritual, or exchange.

4. Select two students to role-play this encounter while you deliver the speech. Inform the class about the intended audience. The student role-players should *literally* demonstrate every step of the process.

5. The rest of the class should listen carefully to see if the process was clear and to see if the speech structure was followed. The class should discuss each presentation.

Library Research Assignment for Collecting and Analyzing Supporting Material

CHAPTER 3: RESEARCH AND REASONING

Objectives

- To learn more about the process of a library search strategy, from topic selection to analysis of information.

- To become aware of sources of multicultural materials available in a reference library.

- To be guided through the questioning of the evidence that you have collected.

Steps

1. Read "Conducting Library Research" on the following page.

2. Go to the library with your instructor and begin the exercise.

Conducting Library Research

A search strategy is a plan to conduct a search for information. This exercise will assist your search strategy through (1) defining a topic; (2) locating background information; (3) finding information in books, magazines, journals, newspapers and pamphlets; and (4) analyzing your information. Follow the instructions as completely as you can. Feel free to ask the reference librarian for assistance when you need it.

I. Define a topic.

First of all, choose a topic that interests you. It is difficult to do a good job of researching a subject you don't care about. Specialized dictionaries, thesauri, and encyclopedias can assist you in broadening, narrowing, or otherwise defining the scope of your research. Choose one title from each of the groups below and write in the space beneath the group how the source you've chosen can help you in beginning to research a topic.

1. Dictionaries

   The American Heritage Dictionary of the English Language, Third Edition
   The New Dictionary of American Slang
   The New Grove Dictionary of Music and Musicians
   Black's Law Dictionary

2. Encyclopedias

   Academic American Encyclopedia
   World Book Encyclopedia
   The Guide to American Law
   Dictionary of the History of Ideas
   The Illustrated Encyclopedia of Mankind
   The Encyclopedia of Educational Research
   Encyclopedia of World Cultures

3. Other sources can be useful for browsing in a subject field. For instance, you may want to look through some specialized journals to determine the scope of a field or to view what topics are currently popular. Examine the following two sources and tell how they might help you. How do they differ?

   Magazines for Libraries for the General Reader
   Congressional Quarterly Researcher

II. Locate background information.

Textbooks are usually a good source of basic information on a subject. You've probably already noticed that encyclopedias vary in their coverage of a subject; some will give little more than a long definition, but others have fairly lengthy entries with bibliographies. Use the list of specialized encyclopedias in item 2 of this exercise, or ask a reference librarian to help you find another subject encyclopedia that includes bibliographies. The bibliographies listed at the backs of encyclopedias can be quite helpful for getting important background information because they usually represent basic reading on the topic.

4. Write the name of the encyclopedia you are using.

_____

Add the name of the subject you looked up.

_____

List the complete citations (up to three) from an article's bibliography. If your article or encyclopedia does not include one, choose another source.

III. Find information in books, magazines, journals, newspapers, and pamphlets.

You can locate books in the library's on-line catalogs by subject, author, or title. To more effectively use the subject catalog, you should consult the Library of Congress Subject Headings to determine the correct form of heading and any related headings.

5. What is the subject you are looking for?

_____

If your subject is not listed this way in LCSH, how is it listed?

_____

Are related terms (RT) listed? _____ What are they?

_____

Are broader terms (BT) listed? _____ How might these be helpful to you?

_____

_____

6. You should now have a list of several subject headings under which you can find books on your topic in the library. List at least three of these books here, using title, author and call number:

If your search for books in your library is not entirely successful, it could be because your subject is too broad, too narrow, or too new. It could be that your library just doesn't have the books that you need, or that they don't exist. They may be checked out, too simple, too detailed, or in a language you don't read. Often, it can be difficult to find books in interdisciplinary areas through traditional catalogs, and it may be difficult to coordinate subject terms. At this point, you may want to continue your research using computer searches and indexes to periodical literature, or need to ask a librarian for assistance. Ask about interlibrary loan to obtain those books your library does not own.

There are two major ways to locate magazine and journal articles on a particular topic. Indexes to broad subject areas appear on a regular basis on computer and in bound volumes, and allow the researcher to keep track of articles published in a wide variety of magazines and specialized journals. Separate bibliographies generally are published on a one-time basis, are usually compiled by librarians or other scholars, and cover the literature of a fairly specified field.

While some indexes tend to cover magazines, others cover mostly scholarly journals. This distinction cannot always be counted on. It is ultimately up to the researcher to determine the authoritativeness, merit, and validity of the information. It is worth noting here that although indexes and bibliographies cover mostly periodical literature, they may also include citations of books, government documents, conference proceedings, dissertations, and other types of materials.

Choose the appropriate index from each group and look up your topic. Use as many volumes of the index as you need. List at least two complete citations for each group.

7. *ProQuest Periodicals Index*
    Reader's Guide
    Ethnic Newswatch

    a.

    b.

8. *Social Sciences Index*
   Humanities Index
   P.A.I.S.
   Business Periodicals Index
   General Sciences Index
   Education Index

   a.

   b.

9. *Foreign Affairs Fifty-Years Index*
   National Geographic Index
   Scientific American Cumulative Index
   Biography and Genealogy Master Index (CD-ROM)
   American History and Life
   Art Index

   If your subject is not covered by any of the indexes here, ask a reference librarian to show you an index that does include your topic.

   a.

   b.

   Newspaper indexes are used in much the same way as journal indexes to find published articles by subject. Major city newspapers are found in the *ProQuest Newspaper Index*.

10. Choose any two different newspaper sources from the following three groups and list the citations you have located on your topic.

    The New York Times Index
    The Washington Post Index
    ProQuest Newspaper Index

    Pamphlets are another good source of information, especially for current topics. They range from leaflets of a few pages to small booklets, and can contain valuable statistical information. Issued by associations, government agencies, and special pamphlet-publishing companies, they are usually kept in folders arranged alphabetically by subject on the shelves in the Pamphlet File (sometimes referred to as the Vertical File of the library).

11. If the library has pamphlets on a certain subject, they would be contained in the Pamphlet File Subject Index. Check the index on your subject. Are there materials on it?

Name the title of one.

IV.   Analyze your information.

12. Look at the citations you listed for item 7, and find one of the articles in the library. Do the same for item 9. Compare the two articles and the journals in which they were published. What differences do you note?

You can also use resources in the library to locate book reviews when you want another person's opinion of a book's merit and usefulness. Use the library's book review sources to determine appropriate indexes for locating book reviewers' opinions.

Book Review Digest
Book Review Index

V.   Analyze information carefully.

Ask critical questions of the material you read. Don't let yourself always be the victim of others' opinions, biases, and judgments. For your assignments in class, address these issues in particular:

Will this information be of interest to my audience?
Would this supporting material make me appear more credible?

The following questions can also often be helpful when you are analyzing information:

What are the main issues?
What assumptions underlie the conclusions?
Can I define the key terms or phrases? Are they ambiguous?
What are the value conflicts? What assumptions are made about values?
Do I recognize any contradictions?
Are there words or phrases indicating bias, emotional appeals, or propaganda?
What is the evidence? Does it support the conclusion?
For statistics: Are the data adequate? Are samples representative?
     Are measurements valid? Are there flaws in the statistical reasoning?

Are other explanations or conclusions possible?
What are the relationships or associations among the ideas presented?
Am I allowing my own bias to prejudice my research?
Is any significant information omitted?

Remember that libraries do not advocate the ideas found in them. There is a tremendous amount of poorly researched information and a great variety in opinion, values, and interpretations. Remember that facts are not knowledge; you must integrate facts into an intelligent, thoughtful, cohesive presentation of information.

Ethnic and Cultural Library Resources

Background Resources

Encyclopedia of World Cultures
This source provides background understanding before students read of specific incidents in newspapers or magazines.

Harvard Encyclopedia of American Ethnic Groups, 1980.
Though the statistics may be out of date, many aspects of the history and development of cultures are provided.

Guide to Multicultural Resources, 1989.

Statistical Almanacs
Ethnic groups are separately listed.

Cultural and Historical Atlases
Ethnic groups are separately listed.

Library Catalog
Look under "American ethnic groups" for general background information. Specific ethnic-group listings will lead the researcher to both reference books and books available to check out.

Talk to the librarian on duty. Asking for help is likely to yield resources one would not find alone.

Specific Information Resources

Ethnic Newswatch
This is a full-text CD-ROM of articles and editorials from newspapers and magazines with African-American, Arab-American, Asian-American, European and Eastern European, Hispanic/Latino/Chicano, Jewish, and Native American perspectives.

National Newspaper Index
Many large urban newspapers listed here have published articles about cultural perspectives. (Each large newspaper also has its own index.)

Local public library clip files
Most local libraries clip and provide in vertical files articles from local newspapers, including community papers.

Community associations
Ethnic and cultural groups often have association offices. They typically maintain clip files of articles from local papers relevant to their issues.

Newspaper office
Sometimes small newspapers maintain their own indexes to their papers and provide access to them.

Educational Research Information Center (ERIC)
Determine how the ERIC system is accessible in your library. It offers articles on an extensive list of education-related topics.

Via Internet Most college campuses are linked to Internet ERIC systems, providing information on education-related topics. The SUNY libraries provide a particularly useful computerized ERIC database.

Via FirstSearch through the Internet.

Via Silver Platter Silver Platter is an excellent, 1966-to-present, CD-ROM ERIC system that is easy to use.

Via Dialog Dialog is a fast CD-ROM ERIC system.

Bound in volumes

Public Affairs Information Service Bulletin (PAIS) PAIS is a social sciences index which lists books, pamphlets, and periodicals.

Cross Cultural CD via Silver Platter This CD-ROM program indexes social and behavioral sciences topics, indexing over 1,000 books and articles, within ten topical databases.

National Geographic Index
Though *National Geographic* is included in most magazine indexes, looking at the magazine's own index can help the reader recognize the cultural angle of topics. This source is a dependable one for in-depth information.

Social Science Index

Humanities Index

Resources on Specific Cultures

African American   (See Library of Congress listings E184 and E185.)

African-American Culture and History, 1995.

Bibliographic Guide to Black Studies, Annual.

Black Americans Information Directory, Biennial.
Includes organizations, newspapers, newsletters, and videos.

Dictionary of Black Culture

Encyclopedia of Black America, 1981.

In Black and White: A Guide to Magazine Articles, Newspaper Articles and Books Concerning More Than 15,000 Black Individuals and Groups, 1980.

Index to Black Periodicals, Annual.

Statistical Record of Black Americans, Annual.

Asian American (See Library of Congress listing E184.)

Asian Americans Information Directory
Includes organizations, newspapers, newsletters, and videos, listed by Asian nationality.

Guide to Establishing Core Collections in Asian American Studies

Statistical Record of Asian Americans, Annual.

Hispanic-American (See Library of Congress listing E184.)

Anuario Hispano: Hispanic Yearbook

The Hispanic American Almanac: A Reference Work on Hispanics in the United States

Hispanic Americans Information Dictionary
Includes organizations, newspapers, newsletters, and videos, listed by Hispanic nationality.

Jewish American (See Library of Congress listing E184.)

Jewish-American History and Culture: An Encyclopedia

Native American Indian (See Library of Congress listing E77.)

Encyclopedia of Native American Tribes, 1988.
Beginning level alphabetical listing of 150 tribes in North America, covering culture, present and historical.

Native Americans: An Annotated Bibliography, 1991.

Thanks to Susan H. Roth, Associate Professor, Library, Prince George's Community College, Largo, MD, and Ann Masnik, Reference Librarian, Hornbake Library, University of Maryland, College Park, MD, for their assistance in compiling this bibliographic list.

Perceptions Versus Realities

CHAPTER 3: RESEARCH AND REASONING

Objectives

- To increase your understanding that "common knowledge" may not be factually accurate.

- To increase your willingness to test information before believing it.

Steps

1. Read the following statistics to the class:

- One out of six American blacks was in the middle class in 1950, compared to four out of six today.

- More than 25 percent of American blacks have attended college.

- In 1989, proportionately more white, non-Hispanic males dropped out of school than black females.

- The average American poor family is one headed by a single, white female parent.[1]

- The precise scope of the Nazi persecution of gay men and lesbians is not known. It is estimated that between 1933 and 1945, 90,000 to 100,000 were arrested; 50,000 to 60,000 sentenced to prison; and 10,000 to 15,000 incarcerated in concentration camps.[2]

- In a Time/CNN poll of 18- to 29-year-olds, 65% of those surveyed agreed it will be harder for their group to live as comfortably as previous generations. While the majority of today's young adults think they have a strong chance of finding a well-paying and interesting job, 69% believe they will have more difficulty buying a house, and 52% say they will have less leisure time than their predecessors. Asked to describe their generation, 53% said the group is worried about the future.[3]

[1]*The Washington Post*, June 21, 1992, sec. C, p. 1.

[2]*The Washington Post*, June 6, 1994, sec. D, pp. 1 and 4.

[3]*Time*, July 16, 1990, p. 58.

- "If you live in New Mexico, California, Hawaii, New York or the District of Columbia, there is a greater than 50 percent chance that any two individuals you encounter will differ ethnically or racially."[4]

- In 1992, 76% of new immigrants entered the U.S. legally, 24% entered illegally. A 1993 survey found that Americans believed that only 24% were legal and 64% illegal.[5]

- The 1990 census showed that almost 25% of Americans have an African, Asian, Hispanic or Native American heritage.[6]

2. Discuss ways in which these statistics seem contrary to "common beliefs."

3. Share other commonly-believed "facts" that may be questionable (as, "most . . ." or "all . . ." statements).

4. Discuss ways to research the statistical answers to those issues.

5. Identify a "common knowledge" assumption you have believed was true. Research this belief, and come back to class with some documentation to support or challenge that belief.

[4] *National Education Association Today*, September 1992, p. 8.

[5] *Time, Special Issue: The New Face of America*, Fall 1993, p. 10.

[6] *The New York Times*, March 11, 1991, p. A1.

Organizing the Speech

CHAPTER 4: ORGANIZATION

Objectives

- To appreciate an alternative organizational approach to writing a speech.

- To provide the basis for class discussion of alternative organizational patterns to linear Western reasoning.

Steps

1. Read "The Speech of Red Jacket," which begins on the following page.

2. Discuss as a class the order in which the speaker presents evidence and claims. Consider the way some cultures ground their public communication in the context of their spiritual beliefs.

3. Discuss the way in which the Great Spirit's presence and impact is the primary topic; the nature of the universe is clarified before specific topics are discussed.

4. Discuss the primary and secondary purposes of the speech. Consider the way the primary goal, to explain that he will postpone any decisions about converting to Christianity, is not introduced until very late in the speech.

5. Additionally, use the speech to illustrate language selection, use of metaphor and repetition, and speaker style.

The Speech of Red Jacket: An Example of Alternative Speech Organization

How to organize our thoughts into clear communication is something we have been taught since elementary school. It is easy to forget that, like everything else we learn, the way we create clear communication is influenced by our culture. That is, an American perception of an effective speech could differ greatly from what other cultures perceive as most effective.

Our speech textbooks teach linear organization, clear purpose, clear distinct parts of the body of the speech that make up the whole, without repetition. But in other cultures, speeches may suggest topics indirectly rather than directly. Issues are raised, left behind, then returned to later in the speech. Consider the following example of non-Western speech organization.

Red Jacket was a Seneca chief living in what is now Seneca County, New York, from 1758 to 1830. He was described as a talented orator, with dramatic organization, effective argument, and skillful presentation. In 1824 he was successful in insisting on the removal of missionaries from Seneca tribal areas. Yet at his death in 1830, his family, who had converted to Christianity, buried Red Jacket with a Christian funeral in a Christian cemetery. These actions were contrary to his expressed wishes. (*Dictionary of American Biography*, s.v. "Red Jacket.")

SPEECH OF RED JACKET

Friend and brother, it was a will of the Great Spirit that we should meet together this day. He orders all things and he has given us a fine day for our council. He has taken his garment from before the sun and has caused a bright orb to shine with brightness upon us. Our eyes are open so that we see clearly. Our ears are unstopped so that we have been able to distinctly hear the words which you have spoken. For all these favors we thank the Great Spirit, and him only.

Brother, this council fire was kindled by you. It was at your request that we came together at this time. We have listened with attention to what you have said. You have requested us to speak our minds freely. This gives us great joy for we now consider that we stand upright before you and can speak what we think. All have heard your voice and all speak to you as one man. Our minds are agreed.

Brother, you say that you want an answer to your talk before you leave this place. It is right that you should have one as you are a great distance from home and we do not wish to detain you. That we will first look back a little, and tell you what our fathers have told us, and what we have heard from the white people.

Brother, listen to what we say. There was a time when our forefathers owned this great island. Their seats extended from the rising to the setting of the sun. The Great Spirit had made it for the use of the Indians. He had created the buffalo, the deer and other animals for food. He made the bear and the deer and their skins served us for clothing. He had scattered them over the country and had taught us how to take them. He had caused the earth to produce corn for bread. All this he had done for his red children because he loved them. If we had any disputes about hunting grounds, they were generally settled without the shedding of much blood.

But an evil day came upon us. Your forefathers crossed the great waters and landed on this island. Their numbers were small. They found friends and not enemies. They told us they had fled from their own country for fear of wicked men and had come here to enjoy their religion. They asked for a small sit. We took pity on them, granted their request and sat down amongst them. We gave them corn and meat, they gave us poison in return. The white people had now found our country. Tidings were carried back and more came amongst us. Yet we did not fear them. We took them to be friends. They called us brothers. We believed them and gave them a large seat. At length their numbers had greatly increased.

They wanted more land. They wanted our country. Our eyes were opened and our minds became uneasy. Wars took place. Indians were hired to fight against Indians and many of our people were destroyed. They also brought strong liquors among us. It was strong and powerful and has slain thousands.

Brother, our seats were once large and yours very small. You have now become a great people and we have scarcely place left to spread our blankets. You have got our country but you are not satisfied. You want to force your religion upon us.

Brother, continue to listen. You say that you are sent to instruct us how to worship the Great Spirit agreeable to his mind and if we do not take hold of the religion which you white people teach, we shall be unhappy hereafter. You say that you are right and we are lost. How do you know this to be true? We understand that your religion is written in a book. If it was intended for us as well as for you why has not the Great Spirit given it to us? And not only to us, but why did he not give to our forefathers knowledge of that book with the means of understanding it rightly? We only know what you tell us about it. How shall we know when to believe, being so often deceived by the white man?

Brother, you say there is but one way to worship and serve the Great Spirit. If there is but one religion why do you white people differ so much about it? Why not all agree as you can all read the book. Brother, we do not understand these things.

We are told that your religion was given to your forefathers and has been handed down father to son. We also have a religion which was given to our forefathers and has been handed down to us, their children. We worship that way. It teaches us to be thankful for all the favors we receive, to love each other and to be united. We never quarrel about religion.

Brother, the Great Spirit has made us all. But he has made a great difference between his white and red children. He has given us a different complexion and different customs.

To you he has given the arts. To these he has not opened our eyes. We know these things to be true. Why may not we conclude that he has given us a different religion?

The Great Spirit does right. He knows what is best for his children. We are satisfied. Brother, we do not wish to destroy your religion or to take it from you. We only want to enjoy our own. Brother, you say you have not come to get our land or our money but to enlighten our minds. I will now tell you that I have been at your meeting and saw you collecting money from the meeting. I can't tell what this money was intended for but suppose it was for your minister and if we should conform to your way of thinking perhaps you may want some from us.

Brother, we are told that you are preaching to the white people in this place. These people are our neighbors. We are acquainted with them. We will wait a little while and see what effect your preaching has upon them. If we find it does them good and makes them honest and less disposed to cheat Indians, we will then consider again what you have said.

Brother, you have now heard our answer to your talk and this is all we have to say at present. As we are going to part, we will come and take you by the hand and hope the Great Spirit will protect you on your journey and return you safe to your friends.

Source: Arthur Junaluska, ed. *Great American Indian Speeches*, Vol. 1, audiotape (New York: HarperCollins Publishers, Inc., 1976).

Speech Mapping

CHAPTER 4: ORGANIZATION

Objectives

- To understand an alternative way to organize a speech.

- To assist visual learners in the steps to organizing a speech.

Steps

1. Speech mapping is an alternative way to organize a speech by visually diagramming its parts.

2. Practice making a speech map following the handout, "Speech Mapping."

3. Encourage those who like being able to see the branches of the speech in this way to create a map, then develop an outline from the map.

Speech Mapping

A map contains five elements: thesis, major points, subpoints, introduction, and conclusion. Design it as a tree fallen on its side, with trunk on the left, branches on the right. The trunk represents the thesis, telling the focus of the speech; the branches are the major points that will be the parts of the speech.

For example:

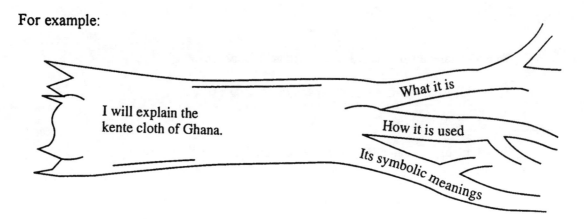

Major points can then be further divided into subpoints.

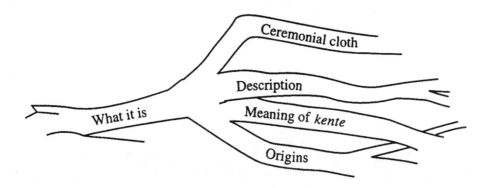

The introduction and conclusion can then be added to the left side of the tree, independent of the branching.

Ethics

CHAPTER 5: CREDIBILITY AND ETHICS

Objectives

- To introduce the concept of communication ethics.

- To introduce students to the instructor's standards for classroom ethics.

- To discuss the role of culture in determining what we consider ethical behavior.

Steps

1. Break the class into small groups of students.

2. Hand each group's members Case One, Case Two, or Case Three and have the students read through the material. Each situation asks the students to come to some agreement about which action they feel is an appropriate response.

3. Have a spokesperson from each group report decisions to the class. Discuss the choices and the reasons for them.

*INSTRUCTOR: See Exercise Notes for this exercise in the back of the book.

Case One

Read the three situations. Your group is to try to come to agreement about the appropriate action to be taken by a college student in each situation.

Situation one: You put off doing your speech until the last minute. A student who completed speech class the semester before offers to sell you the speech she researched and gave the previous semester (earning a grade of A). What would you do?

Situation two: A student gives in class an antigay speech that claims that gay men typically molest young boys. After the speech, what would you do?

Situation three: You work with five other students preparing and organizing your in-class, researched symposium. The professor erroneously believes one particular student did the agenda and most of the research, and praises only that student. In reality you did most of the work. What would you do? (Assume no one else in the group speaks up.)

Case Two

You work for the More Suds Soap Company. This company has a line of cleaning products it sells all over the world. One particular soap is a top-selling laundry soap. This product was "improved" so that the company could market it as a better cleaner.

The company changed the packaging and has marketed the product heavily. Customers are staying loyal and are buying the new product. After the product is on the market for a short time, the Environmental Protection Agency discovers that the new ingredients added to the soap to improve it interact with the other chemicals in the soap—making it a pollutant, difficult if not impossible to break down in the water treatment process.

The Environmental Protection Agency (EPA) requires the soap company to withdraw its new product and stop the use of the new additives.

The company has agreed to cooperate with haste in withdrawing the product, provided they are allowed to handle the public relations of this decision without the EPA's publicizing its report on the polluting nature of the product.

Suppose your group is meeting to set the course for handling the public statement of the company. You have a variety of choices, including pulling the product and telling the American public the truth, pulling the product and selling it overseas to recoup some of your losses, changing the product back to its original form and telling no one, or inventing some other reason for the change in products. There are other possible choices as well.

Select the approach you think is best. Then decide what the public message would be, how it would best be communicated, and whom you would appoint as spokesperson.

Case Three

A speaker for an international AIDS research foundation decides to purposefully exaggerate the statistics on one's chances of getting AIDS. He or she is speaking at a huge fundraiser for international AIDS research.

The speaker believes in the greater good. An audience that is more fearful will donate more for research and more people will be helped.

Do you think the speaker is making the right choice in this situation?

Credibility in a Multicultural Society

CHAPTER 5: CREDIBILITY AND ETHICS

Objectives

- To identify the cultural elements of credibility in persuasive speaking.

- To identify culture biases in the perceived credibility of public speakers.

Steps

1. Read the excerpt on "credibility," from *An Introduction to Intercultural Communication*, by Condon and Yousef (on the following page).

2. Discuss the following questions in class:

   a. Are there ways which a person may enhance his or her credibility that stem from cultural background? What might some of these ways be?

   b. Are there biases within your culture that may affect your personal credibility? In what ways might these biases work in your favor? In what ways might they work against you?

   c. On which speech topics would you be perceived as highly credible? Is there a particular audience that you should address on this topic?

Speaker Competence from a Global Perspective

"As a general principle the ethos of the speaker may universally be the most important factor in persuasiveness. However, what constitutes good **ethos** is not necessarily universal. . . [V]alue orientations will give the best guidance for discovering the ideal ethos of a particular culture. In many societies age will be crucial: The best ethos may accrue to one who is over sixty or under forty. Sex may be crucial: in many societies women are believed to be competent to speak only of women's matters. Family background, achievement, education, relation to the military, religion, and more are likely to be constituents of ethos. As these will differ from culture to culture, their influence in intercultural communication should be obvious."

Source: John C. Condon and Fathi Yousef, *An Introduction to Intercultural Communication* (Indianapolis: The Bobbs-Merrill Company, Inc., 1975), p. 246.

Establishing Credibility with My Class Audience

CHAPTER 5: CREDIBILITY AND ETHICS

Objectives

- To recognize that each audience establishes its own definition of "credible."

- To determine what factors would increase speaker credibility with your particular audience.

Steps

1. Fill out the questionnaire on the following page.

2. In pairs or a small group, determine how similar your responses were to those of other students.

3. Discuss what observations that you have made about each other might have led you to these conclusions.

4. Discuss ways each of you as speakers might adapt to what the audience perceives as credible.

Class Credibility Factors

Answer the questions below to reflect your view of attitudes held by your public speaking class. Circle a number, 1–5, to indicate your view of how important an item would be in establishing strong positive credibility. Make 1 least important and 5 most important. Numbers can be used as often as needed.

1.	Military experience	1	2	3	4	5
2.	Volunteer experience	1	2	3	4	5
3.	Wall Street work experience	1	2	3	4	5
4.	Farming experience	1	2	3	4	5
5.	Sales experience	1	2	3	4	5
6.	Having lived in another country	1	2	3	4	5
7.	Being under 30 years old	1	2	3	4	5
8.	Being over 60 years old	1	2	3	4	5
9.	Being a parent	1	2	3	4	5
10.	Being raised by a wealthy family	1	2	3	4	5
11.	Having experienced an abortion	1	2	3	4	5
12.	Wearing clothing that is very stylish	1	2	3	4	5
13.	Being an alcoholic in recovery	1	2	3	4	5
14.	Having experience in local politics	1	2	3	4	5

Cultural Differences in the Emotional Component of Public Speaking

CHAPTER 6: EMOTIONAL APPEAL

Objectives

- To recognize differences in expectations of speakers held by audiences from different cultures.

- To increase awareness of the unique role of words in African tradition.

- To analyze the appropriate uses of emotional appeal in various speaking situations.

Steps

1. Read the following passages:

   The modes of behavior that blacks and whites consider appropriate for engaging in public debate on an issue differ in their stance and level of spiritual intensity. The black mode—that of black community people—is high-keyed: animated, interpersonal, and confrontational. The white mode—that of the middle class—is relatively low-keyed: dispassionate, impersonal, and non-challenging. The first is characteristic of involvement; it is heated, loud, and generates affect. The second is characteristic of detachment and is cool, quiet, and without affect.[1]

   In African American culture, as in other oral cultures, communication is direct and immediate. One has to act and react spontaneously, because there is instantaneous feedback. . . There is no distinction made between the "speaker" and the "audience." The communication that transpires between them is the "creation and sharing of one's personhood."[2]

2. Discuss the implications for speakers when
   a. the audience is comfortable with highly-engaged discussion.
   b. the audience is comfortable with detached presentation.

   In what ways could speakers adapt to these differences?

[1]Thomas Kochman, *Black and White Styles in Conflict* (Chicago: University of Chicago Press, 1981), pp. 18–19.

[2]Thurmon Garner, "Oral Rhetorical Practice in African American Culture," in *Our Voices: Essays in Culture, Ethnicity, and Communication* (Los Angeles: Roxbury Publishing Company, 1994), p. 81.

3. Keep in mind that every member of a culture cannot be expected to follow the norms of that culture. Historical family and current personal preferences make individuals impossible to predict.

   Clearly, not all white audience members and all African American audience members demonstrate the extremes of Kochman's examples. Class differences as well as race differences are described here. Try not to get sidetracked by the generalization of highly-charged African Americans and dispassionate whites. Research supports it, but of course it is not always true.

4. Depending on the cultural experiences and background of your class, discuss other cultures that have an oral tradition like those of many African cultures.

Traditional American Values

CHAPTER 6: EMOTIONAL APPEAL

Objectives

- To determine what might be some traditional American values.

- To determine to what traditional American values you might wish to appeal in your persuasive speech topic.

Steps

1. Read through the list of some traditional American values on the sheet that follows.

2. Go back through the list and check off three or four values that you think could be appropriate appeals with the topic you have selected for your persuasive speech assignment.

3. At the bottom of the page briefly explain why you believe those values are reflected in your speech topic.

Traditional American Values Worksheet

It is valuable to:

_____ Get ahead.	_____ Help your fellow man.
_____ Be honest.	_____ Be tolerant.
_____ Participate in government.	_____ Explore.
_____ Work hard.	_____ Win.
_____ Be clean.	_____ Look out for yourself.
_____ Honor one's parents.	_____ Obey the law.
_____ Be loyal to your country.	_____ Influence other countries to become democratic.
_____ Live.	_____ Be partisan.
_____ Be free.	_____ Know your heritage.
_____ Pursue happiness.	_____ Build things.
_____ Accrue goods and wealth.	_____ Save time.
_____ Become educated.	_____ Find a better way.
_____ Be religious.	_____ Be proud of your city, state, section.
_____ Know the right people.	_____ Adjust to the prevailing social norms.
_____ Live in the right places.	_____ Stand up for what you think is right.
_____ Be productive.	

How do traditional values relate to my persuasive speech subject?

Source: Reproduced from *The 1973 Annual Handbook for Group Facilitators*, by J. E. Jones and J. W. Pfeiffer (eds.). Copyright ©1973 by Pfeiffer & Company, San Francisco, CA. Used with permission.

Universal Values

CHAPTER 6: EMOTIONAL APPEAL

Objective

- To consider shared universal values and how you might reflect those values in your speeches.

Steps

1. Read the list of universal values on the page that follows. The Schwartz study confirmed that people in a large number of cultures distinguish 10 types of values when evaluating the importance of concrete values as guiding their life principles. ". . . the power, achievement, and tradition types were universal, as they emerged in all countries. The hedonism, self-direction, universalism, and security types were found in 95% of countries, and the stimulation, benevolence, and conformity types were found in 90% of countries."[3] This study used data from 20 different countries, speaking 13 different languages, represented by 8 major religions and atheists, and was occupationally centered on school teachers and university students.

2. Select which universal values might be reflected in your persuasive speech. Write a description of how you might reflect in your speech each value selected.

3. Break into small groups and discuss your findings.

[3]Shalom H. Schwartz, "Universals in the Content and Structure of Values: Theoretical Advances and Empirical Tests in 20 Countries," *Advances in Experimental Social Psychology*, vol. 25, 1992, p. 38.

Universal Values Worksheet

NAME _____ **SPEECH TOPIC** _____

SELF-DIRECTION

STIMULATION

HEDONISM

ACHIEVEMENT

POWER

SECURITY

CONFORMITY

TRADITION

BENEVOLENCE

UNIVERSALISM

See Shalom H. Schwartz, "Universals in the Content and Structure of Values: Theoretical Advances and Empirical Tests in 20 Countries," *Advances in Experimental Social Psychology*, vol. 25, 1992, pp. 1–65.

Interest Letters

CHAPTER 6: EMOTIONAL APPEAL

Objectives

- To demonstrate the various persuasive techniques used in support of a relevant social issue.

- To demonstrate the potential for audience empowerment.

- To encourage your use of critical thinking techniques and evaluative listening.

- To aid you in topic selection.

Steps

1. Your instructor will provide an interest letter that deals with a relevant contemporary issue: i.e., a letter from the World Wildlife Fund, Mothers Against Drunk Driving, or the National Gay and Lesbian Task Force.

2. Read the letter and circle the persuasive appeals that are present.

*INSTRUCTOR: See Exercise Notes for this exercise in the back of the book.

Beware of American Idioms

CHAPTER 7: PRESENTATION

Objectives

- To increase awareness of idioms in my own speech.

- To practice replacing idioms with words that might be more universally understood.

Steps

1. Read over the list of idioms on the following page.

2. Check those you might use as a speaker. Add others to the list that you use.

3. Star those you would not understand if you were an audience member.

4. With a partner, discuss better alternatives that Americans might use for some of the idioms on the list.

American English Idioms

100K (for 100,000)
All your eggs in one basket
Bases are loaded
Bite the dust
Blow off steam
Chip on your shoulder
Dog and pony show
Downtime
Fed up
Fourth and ten situation
Get your feet wet.
It will never fly.
Keep your shirt on.
Land on your feet
On a roll
On the same wavelength
Overview
Read between the lines.
Run it up the flagpole.
Scratch that plan.
Shotgun approach
Time to punt
You scratch my back and I'll scratch yours.
You've barely scratched the surface.

_____

_____

_____

_____

Adapted from Roger E. Axtell, *Do's and Taboos Around the World*, 2nd ed. (New York: John Wiley & Sons, Inc., 1990), p. 158, and Lisa M. Skow, Karen E. Zediker and Larry A. Samovar, *Instructor's Resource Manual for Samovar and Porter's Intercultural Communication*, 7th ed. (Belmont, CA: Wadsworth Publishing Company, 1994), p. 115.

Nonverbal Taboos

CHAPTER 7: PRESENTATION

Objectives

- To increase awareness of positive and negative nonverbal actions of speakers.

- To increase awareness of cultural differences in gestures and delivery across cultures.

Steps

1. Working in a small group, generate a list of nonverbal gestures, facial expressions, body movements, etc., that would usually seem inappropriate to an American audience. For example, shaking a finger in the face of an audience member, eyes to the ceiling, turning one's back to the audience for a length of time, talking longer than the time prescribed.

2. Find out which group members have lived in other parts of the United States or in other countries. Share examples of nonverbal communication members have observed that is different from local customs.

Impromptu Speech Topics

CHAPTER 8: IMPROMPTU

Objective

- To practice impromptu speaking on topics related to multicultural issues.

Steps

1. Each of you will draw two or three impromptu topics provided by your instructor. Then choose your preference.

2. Each speech should include a clear statement of the topic as it is written, and a clear response to that topic. Introductions and conclusions may be optional.

Impromptu Topics

One group I choose to affiliate with and why.

A family gathering with special significance for me.

A cultural group I believe is misunderstood.

Is abortion dividing America?

Fight AIDS, help people.

Hate is not a family value.

When I was younger, I dreamed about being a. . . .

I wish that men/women wouldn't. . . .

One family saying that is important to me is. . . .

The funniest bumper sticker I ever saw.

The family renegade was. . . .

Something I was told as a child that made me angry.

One group I admire and why.

One place I'd like to visit and why.

Who's marching on Washington?

Practice random acts of kindness.

Good things happen.

The best thing about my hometown is. . . .

I wish there was more news reporting about. . . .

Something important I learned about myself is. . . .

Insured by Smith and Wesson.

A woman's place is in the House . . . and the Senate.

My kid can beat up your honor roll kid.

If you don't stand for something, you'll fall for anything.

Informative Speech Topics with Cultural Emphasis

CHAPTER 9: INFORMATIVE SPEAKING

Objective

- To explore multicultural topics.

Steps

1. At the beginning of classroom instruction on informative speaking, read the "Informative Speech Topics" list.

2. Get into small groups to discuss topics on the list that interest you. Give each feedback on the audience's amount of knowledge and of attitudes toward those topics. How might the speaker need to adapt?

Informative Speech Topics

Edible Insects
Rosa Parks
Cultural Taboos
The Persons with Disabilities Act:
    What Does It All Mean?
Rosh Hashana
Diversity Training in the Workplace
Political Correctness in Language
Ramadan
African-American/Jewish-American Relations
Salza Music
The Chicano View of the Alamo
College Entrance Criteria
Genealogy
Increasing the Number of Choices of
    Official Racial and Ethnic
    Categories Set by the
    Federal Government
Mexican Vaqueros, the Original Cowboys
The Chinese Pictographic Alphabet
Afrocentric Education
The Significance of Hopi Kachina
The Rise of Fidel Castro
Wilderness Camps for Troubled Teenagers
Arranged Marriages
Ethnic Tensions in Western Russia
Same-Sex Marriage Ceremonies
What Are Different Forms of Education
    for the Deaf?

Love and Romance After 55
Soul Food
Stonewall: The Beginning of a Movement
The Effect in the Workplace of Cultural
    Variations of Time and Space
The Japanese Educational System
Baha'i
Salvador Dali
Attention Deficit Disorder
Reggae
Geronimo
Effects of the Supreme Court's Rejection of
    Congressional Districts Created to
    Increase Representation of People of Color
The Black Cowboy—Well-Represented in the
    Old West
The Building of the U.S. Railroads
The Difficulties Faced by Amerasians
    in Vietnam After the War
Barrio Life in the Early 1900s
The Influence of Cuban Culture on Florida
The Cherokees' Trail of Tears
Mayan Archeological Remains
Palestinian Culture
Internet Addiction
The Japanese Concept of Gaman
The Power of Words in West African Tradition
Polygamy
Hate Crimes

Informative Sample Speeches

CHAPTER 9: INFORMATIVE SPEAKING

Objective

- To understand examples of adapting a non-American topic to the classroom speech assignment.

Steps

1. Read the "The Significance of the Kente Cloth of Ghana, West Africa" and "The Jewish-Arab Conflict" speech outlines.

2. Discuss the ways in which global or other cultural diversity topics can be developed, using typical informative outline formats.

The Significance of the Kente Cloth of Ghana, West Africa

INTRODUCTION

It has been said that "clothes make the man." But much more than in United States culture, in Ghana, West Africa, a cloth called *kente* symbolically communicates a great deal about the man or woman who wears it.

PURPOSE

Today I want to teach you about the unique ceremonial cloth of Ghana, the kente cloth.

CENTRAL IDEA

I will explain what *kente* is, its usage, and its symbolic meanings.

BODY

A.   What is a *kente* cloth?
1. It is a ceremonial cloth from the Asante region of Ghana, West Africa.
2. It is handwoven.
3. Its description is as follows:
    a.   It consists of strips about four inches wide.
    b.   These are sewn together into larger pieces of cloth.
4. The term *kente* means "basket." The first weavers used cloths that looked like woven baskets.
5. The origins of the *kente* suggest it is very old.
    a.   The tradition dates to 3000 B.C.
    b.   Asante people developed the technique in the seventeenth century.

B.   The uses of the *kente* always suggest the prestigious status of wearing it.
1. The original use was for royalty only.
2. It is now associated with wealth, high social status, and cultural sophistication.
3. There is usually a sacred intent to its use.
4. It is often a gift on special occasions.
    a.   Child naming
    b.   Puberty
    c.   Graduation
    d.   Marriage
    e.   Soul-washing
    f.   Burial
5. It is also worn for festive occasions.
    a.   Celebrations
    b.   Historic events

6. It is worn in different ways.

    a. Men usually wear one piece wrapped around the body, right shoulder uncovered, togalike style.

    b. Women wear either one large piece, or two to three six-foot-long pieces. They wrap kente around their bodies with or without a matching blouse.

    c. Elderly women wear it togalike style, as men do.

    d. Age, marital status, and social standing may determine the size and design worn.

    e. Modern ways are varying the uses of the *kente*.

C. *Kente* patterns have symbolic meaning.

    1. The pattern of the motif has symbolic meaning; there are more than 42 motifs.

        a. One example is the star pattern. It symbolizes the female essence of life, faithfulness, and affection.

        b. Another example is the fingers pattern, with four thick horizontal lines. Fingers are seen as a practical expression of human thought, so this pattern symbolizes practicality, dignity of labor, and creativity.

    2. The pattern in which motifs are arranged into cloths has symbolic meaning; there are more than 54 cloth patterns. In them two or more patterns are checkerboarded together.

        a. One example is Adwinasa.

            1) It is an attempt to use all motifs, so is considered most prestigious.

            2) It symbolizes royalty and elegance.

        b. Another example is Kyeretwie.

            1) It means "the lion catcher."

            2) It commemorates the reign of King Kwaku Dua, 1838–67, who tested the courage of warriors by requiring them to catch a leopard live.

            3) The black stripes represent the black spots of a leopard. The cloth symbolizes courage.

CONCLUSION

Before my speech you may have thought this was just a pretty piece of yellow cloth (showing a kente). Now you know it communicates an important message. It is the Nkasewa, and I hope you all earn the right to wear it. It symbolizes finesse in public speaking.

Source: Kwaku Ofori-Ansa, *Kente Is More Than a Cloth: History and Significance of Ghana's Kente Cloth*, Poster (Hyattsville, MD: San Kofa Publications, 1993).

The Jewish-Arab Conflict

By Hagit Barrett

INTRODUCTION

In Genesis 12:1, almost 4,000 years ago, "The Lord had said to Abraham, 'Leave your country, your people . . . and go to the land I will show you.'" During that time the land was known as Canaan and was located between the Jordan River and the Mediterranean Sea. Since Abraham is the father of two great religions, Islam and Judaism, it was this event that caused both Jews and Arabs to claim this land as their own.

PURPOSE

Today I want to inform you of the background of the conflict between Jews and Arabs for the land.

CENTRAL IDEA

I will describe events before, during, and after the establishment of what is now known as Israel.

BODY

A. The conflict before the establishment of Israel.
   1. Late 1800s to early 1900s Jews immigrate to Palestine, driven by Zionism.
   2. After World War I Palestine falls under British control.
   3. Jewish immigration continues. Balfour Declaration sets stage for the establishment of a Jewish state in Palestine (1917).
   4. Outset of World War II British publish White Paper.
      a. Ending of Balfour Declaration.
      b. Supporting Arabs.
   5. After World War II British unable to control Palestine; gave United Nations responsibility for the disputed territory (1948).
   6. The U.N. vote to partition Palestine into Arab and Jewish states (1947). Israel declares independence (1948).

B. The conflict during the establishment of Israel.
   1. Israel declares independence—Arabs do not accept partition; Arab armies (Egypt, Syria, Lebanon, Jordan, Saudi Arabia, and Iraq) launch a war against Israel (1948).
   2. Israel wins its war of independence (1948).

C. The conflict after the establishment of Israel.
   1. The organization of the PLO (1964).
   2. Egypt's President Nasser declares intention to destroy Jewish state. Israel launches surprise attack against Arab armies (1967).
   3. Yasser Arafat elected Chairman of the PLO (1969).
   4. Syria and Egypt launch surprise attack on Israel (1973).
   5. Peace agreement between Egypt and Israel signed (1979).
   6. The "Intifada" started (1982).

CONCLUSION

Today Israel has a 17-year-old peace agreement with Egypt and a recently completed peace agreement with the PLO and with Jordan. Peace negotiations with Syria ceased after several bus bombings in Israel earlier this year. A lot is being done in the name of peace but there is still much to do. Although the conflict between Jews and Arabs is old, and the peace agreements between them fragile and new, one day the children of Abraham, Jews and Arabs, will end this conflict and live peacefully as brothers in the promised land.

BIBLIOGRAPHY

Dan, Uri. *To the Promised Land.* New York: Doubleday, A Division of Bantam Doubleday Dell Publishing Group Inc., 1988.

Friedman, Thomas L. *From Beirut to Jerusalem.* Toronto: Collins Publishers, 1989.

Metz, Helen Chapin, ed. *The Study of Israel.* Federal Research Division, Library of Congress. (1990).

Naamani, Israel T. *The State of Israel.* New York: Behrman House Inc., 1980.

Safran, Nadav. *Israel The Embattled Ally.* Cambridge, MA: The Belknap Press of Harvard University Press, 1978.

Tessler, Mark. *A History of the Israeli-Palestinian Conflict.* Bloomington: Indiana University Press, 1994.

Tiger Media, Inc., "Lines in the Sand" Internet Home Page (http://www.tiger.ab.ca/mideast).

Persuasive Speech Topics with Cultural Emphasis

CHAPTER 10: PERSUASIVE SPEAKING

Objective

- To explore multicultural topics.

Steps

1. At the beginning of classroom instruction on persuasive speaking, read the "Persuasive Speech Topics" list from the following page.

2. Gather into small groups to discuss topics on the list that interest you. Give one another feedback on the types of audience views they might expect to face on those topics. How might the speaker need to adapt to those views?

Persuasive Speech Topics

Native Americans should be granted exclusive state gambling licenses.

The United States should be at the forefront of worldwide humanitarian relief efforts.

American mass marketing of the kente cloth is disrespectful.

Same-sex marriages should be legal.

Title IX federal guidelines for athletics have harmed many established college sports programs.

Quotas for admission to college are necessary to create a culturally diverse campus.

Professional sports teams should eliminate racist names, mascots, and symbols.

Clandestine military drug testing should be eliminated.

Public schools should not require the mainstreaming of *all* children with disabilities.

Assisted suicide should be legal.

English-only state laws do not discriminate.

The United States should not invade other nations (such as Haiti) when asked to reestablish legitimately elected governments to power.

The workplace should take greater responsibility for supporting employee family care needs.

The United States should not increase the numbers of refugees allowed into the country.

Secondary schools and colleges should address the high dropout rate among Latinos.

More people of color should be hired for front-office jobs in professional sports.

There should be mandatory driving tests for older Americans.

African-American death row inmates should be allowed to use racial discrimination as a defense.

A mandatory retirement age is desirable.

Post-menopausal women should not bear children.

Funding for research on women's diseases should be increased.

National Endowment for the Arts funding should not censor artistic expression.

Future space exploration should be characterized by increased global participation.

The United States should be committed to the role of negotiator for peace in world crises.

Juveniles and adults should be housed separately in prisons.

The United States should not tie trade decisions to other nations' use of child labor.

Gay and lesbian marriages should be recognized in the United States.

Persuasive Sample Speech Outlines

CHAPTER 10: PERSUASIVE SPEAKING

Objective

- To understand examples of adapting a non-American speech topic to the classroom speech assignment.

Steps

1. Read the "Travel to Vietnam" and "Americans Should Support Those Who Flee Female Circumcision" outlines.

2. Discuss the ways in which non-American or other cultural-diversity topics can be developed, using typical persuasive outline formats.

Travel to Vietnam

By Phuong Do

INTRODUCTION

The summer is coming. We are going to finish this semester. Most of you intend to take a vacation.

PURPOSE

I suggest you travel to Vietnam, my country.

CENTRAL IDEA

Many of you indicated that you know very little or nothing about Vietnam. I will analyze this problem, recommend that you visit Vietnam, and explain benefits you gain when you take a vacation in Vietnam.

BODY

    I. Problems

        A. Lack of knowledge about Vietnam

        B. Relations between Vietnam and the United States

        C. The Vietnam war

        D. Cost

    II. Solutions

        A. Learning more about Vietnam

        B. Noting that the United States embargo has been lifted

        C. Realizing that the Vietnam war is long past

        D. Noting that airfares have improved

        E. Going to Vietnam now

III. Benefits

    A. Wonderful scenery

    B. Vietnamese folk music and plays

    C. Delicious food

    D. Beautiful and inexpensive goods

    E. Vietnamese hospitality

    F. Airfare discounts

CONCLUSION

I just identified four reasons why you have not taken a vacation in Vietnam yet, and answered each one. You can enjoy wonderful scenery, Vietnamese music and delicious food, buy great gifts, and get airfare discounts. Travel to Vietnam. Do not miss a chance to enjoy a unique vacation there.

Reprinted by permission of Phuong Do, 1996.

Americans Should Support Those Who Flee Female Circumcision

By Mavis Quarcoo

INTRODUCTION

"I can still visualize the scene and trauma all over again." These are the words of Somali Hassan Farah, recalling when, at the age of eight, she was taken by her mother without warning to be held down and circumcised. In many parts of Africa and Asia, young women still must face this torture.

PURPOSE

Today I want to persuade you that you can help to cease the practice of circumcision against females.

CENTRAL IDEA

I will present you with the problems associated with female circumcision and its effects, then appeal to you to consider some solutions.

BODY

    I. Problems associated with female circumcision

        A. What is done surgically

        B. Who performs circumcisions in different cultures

        C. Reasons for this tradition

    II. Effects of female circumcision

        A. Physical

        B. Psychological/emotional

        C. Social

    III. Solutions

        A. United Nations intervention

        B. American political asylum

        C. Individual education and support

CONCLUSION

Every thousand-mile journey begins with one step. You can start with a decision to do something to help stop this ritual before it gets to your door.

BIBLIOGRAPHY

Fennell, T. "Finding New Grounds for Refuge." *Macleans*, August 8, 1994, pp. 18–19.

Mann, J. "A Welcome Reversal." *The Washington Post*, December 27, 1995, p. 13.

Staff. "Around the World: Female Circumcision Protested." *The Washington Post*, April 13, 1995, p. A22.

Toubia, N. "Female Circumcision as a Public Health Issue." *New England Journal of Medicine*, vol. 332, no. 10, (September 15, 1994), pp. 712–716.

Reprinted by permission of Mavis Quarcoo, 1996.

Persuasive Sample Speech

CHAPTER 10: PERSUASIVE SPEAKING

Objective

- To provide you with an example of adapting a global speech topic to the classroom speech assignment.

Steps

1. Read the "Geographic Illiteracy" speech text.

2. Discuss as a class the ways in which global or other cultural diversity topics can be developed, using typical persuasive outline formats.

Geographic Illiteracy

By Dionne Vincent Spear

"In fourteen-hundred and ninety-two Columbus sailed the ocean blue and found this land, land of the free, beloved by you, beloved by me." Or so the historical rhyme reminds us. According to the National Geographic Society, more than 48 percent of Americans don't know where Columbus landed, and 5 to 15 percent believe that Columbus set sail to find Europe.

Unfortunately, many Americans are geographically illiterate, and few realize just how important geography can be. Geography can be used to assess global environment patterns, to understand international trade, or just to understand the world. In order to further understand geographic illiteracy, let us first discover the significance of the problem; second, explore why it exists; and finally, map out some solutions.

The November 17, 1987, issue of the *Los Angeles Times* reported on a survey conducted by California State University professor William Puzo in which students were told to name and locate the leading trade partner to the United States. The students named Japan, but then none could find it. The leading trade partner to the United States is Canada and only 29 percent of the surveyed students could locate Canada on a map. The survey showed that more than 44 million Americans don't know where the Soviet Union is (was) or the Pacific Ocean. And as for New York, it was placed in 37 different states, from Maine to Florida and from coast to coast.

Finally, across the nation, educators are realizing that Americans are appallingly ignorant of geography. For example, the previously cited survey also told students to locate the United States on a map. One in seven—that's more than 24 million Americans—placed the United States in Australia, or in Botswana, South Africa.

The July 28, 1988, edition of *The New York Times* reported an international Gallup Survey in which young adults, aged 18–24 the world over, were asked to name and locate 16 sites on a map. The Americans scored lowest with fewer than 7 of those 16 sites located. West Germans and Swedes scored the highest with almost 12 of the sites found. Gilbert Grosvenor, president and chairman of the National Geographic Society, in a paper published in July 1985 entitled "What Happens When America Flunks Geography," stated that Americans do not understand geography at a time when they need to understand foreign economic markets, customs, and strengths and weaknesses. He also stated that an ignorance of geography is harmful in that it can deter, frustrate, and finally defeat the best of intentions by all. For example, American ignorance of Vietnam has not lessened, even after U.S. involvement in the Vietnam War. While the Vietnam Veterans Memorial is the most visited memorial in the United States, more than 50 percent of high school graduates cannot locate Vietnam on a map.

Just imagine a banker making international loans without any knowledge of the countries involved, or a doctor treating diseases without understanding the environment where these diseases thrive. At a press conference held at the National Geographic Society headquarters in the fall of 1989, Grosvenor said that "as people we all share the same world . . . if we are to resolve problems such as hunger, global pollution, or nuclear arms control, we must be geographically literate."

So we realize that as a country we know less about world geography than other industrialized nations. According to the educational supplement of the August 3, 1988, edition of *The New York Times*, the problem exists because of a lack of importance placed on the subject in our schools. Only 37 percent of Americans consider learning geography important in order to be a well-educated individual, as compared to 52 percent of Soviets who think that learning the subject is important.

An article in the *Los Angeles Times* (November 9, 1989) reported that geography was phased out of the school curriculum sometime after World War II. As a result only 20 percent of our school educators have ever had classes in geography. A 1988 test designed by C. Warren McKiney to test our future teachers' knowledge of the subject showed that more than 80 percent had no knowledge of geography. McKiney concluded that the only way teachers could teach the subject would be to learn it on the job.

In essence, geography has been lost within the school curriculum. The National Geographic Society believes that it was swallowed and dissolved by social studies, thereby leaving only a handful of states and the District of Columbia to specifically require geography for high school graduation.

If geographic illiteracy is a problem that has to come about simply because the subject is not being taught in our schools, then the solution is education. First, geography can be integrated into the school curriculum once again, but if that is done, it needs to be stated as a specific course objective. That would prevent the subject from being forgotten. So, for example, history teachers would have to teach the geographic significance of some historical event, such as where Christopher Columbus landed and why that is important.

Second, according to a report on education entitled "Geography Education and the United States" published in October 1988, the Council of Chief State Officers believes that the best way to reinstate geography would be to offer workshops for teachers. These workshops would instruct teachers on the importance of geography, what to teach, how to teach it, and how to evaluate their students' achievements.

Finally, geography can be reinstated as a separate subject. This way we can fully realize the advantages a knowledge of geography brings to us. And while concern about Americans' geographical knowledge is not universally shared, Christopher Slater, the chairman of the Geography Department at the University of Missouri, believes that reinstating geography separately is essential in that it "furnishes an understanding of the world, and helps you see the deeper interplay of forces at work within any situation."

We can see the effectiveness of this solution when we look at Heather Hills Elementary School in Bowie, Maryland. Heather Hills Elementary offered workshops for its teachers in early 1990 in which teachers were instructed on the importance of geography and how to teach it to their students. They returned to their classes and taught students how to locate countries on a map, and then discussed the different cultures, histories, native foods, and native dress of those countries. As a result, according to a report aired on September 18, 1990, on ABC News, Heather Hills Elementary School received an award for academic excellence from President Bush.

We also can move across the seas to the former Soviet Union and see the results of its geography education. The Soviets also were administered the Gallup Survey in 1989, but this was given to adults ages 18–24, and age 55 and over. Those 55 and older scored significantly lower than the Americans, but this was because the Soviets in that age group had never had classes in geography. On the other hand, Soviets aged 18–24 scored significantly higher on that survey than the Americans in the same age group. The average Soviet student today has at least seven years of geography classes, compared to American students who have no more than two years, if any.

The impact of geographical illiteracy prompts the question: What can you, as concerned adults, do? First, the National Geographic Society believes that children can benefit if their parents provide them with globes or maps, help them locate countries currently in the news, and discuss not only the impact of events in particular countries but their relation to other countries.

Second, you can become a member of your P.T.A., even if you are not a parent. As an active member, you can interact with teachers, and discuss the importance of geography and why it should be taught to students. Third, talk with school boards and discuss the relevance of the subject and why it should be part of the curriculum. Finally, you can write to the National Education Association and have them act on your behalf in making geography an important and required part in each school's curriculum.

So our explorations have shown that geographic illiteracy exists because the subject is not considered important and is not being taught in our schools. The only solution is education.

President Bush said in 1990 that "when Americans have trouble locating America on the map, it is time to map out a new approach to education." Maybe with this new approach, when we next ask our students where Brussels, Milan, Paris, or the Chesapeake are, they won't answer, "Pepperidge Farm®."

Reprinted by permission of Dionne Vincent Spear, 1996.

Design for Action

CHAPTER 11: ASSESSMENT

Objectives

- To identify a particular multicultural communication issue you wish to improve upon for the benefit of your public speaking.

- To develop a plan for change.

- To make a commitment to action on this issue.

Steps

1. Read the "Design for Action Work Sheet" on the following page.

2. Select a small, manageable multicultural communication issue you wish to improve in, for example, "I wish to become better able as audience member to tolerate English spoken in various accents without being distracted from the message." Provide concrete examples of changes you would like to make.

3. This exercise should be done privately. Your instructor may wish to collect students' papers.

Design For Action Work Sheet

Think about one thing you can do to improve your public speaking or your participation as an effective audience member. Then complete the following action plan for implementing your strategy within the next thirty days.

The problem or issue:

My strategy:

Specific tasks involved. Who will do them and by when?

What are some of the obstacles that may get in the way, and how may I overcome or reduce the impact of each obstacle?

What resources do I need?

How will I demonstrate I have made progress on this issue?

Source: Joe Giordano, lecture presented at Training of Trainers: Developing Cultural Diversity Programs for the Workforce, 1993. Adapted by permission of Joe Giordano, 81 Pondfield Road, Suite #5, Bronxville, NY 10708.

Speaker Self-Evaluation Form

CHAPTER 11: ASSESSMENT

Objectives

- To increase your awareness of cultural influences on public speaking.

- To provide the opportunity for you to analyze the effects of your own speaking style.

Steps

1. Tape record one of your assignments from your speech class.

2. Carefully read through the items on this evaluation sheet before you set out to critique yourself. Watch your speech, commenting on the items suggested below. You may wish to include specific examples from your speech.

Speaker Self-Evaluation Form

NAME _____   **SPEECH TOPIC** _____

SPEAKER ATTITUDES

Was I emotionally involved or more detached as I spoke?

Did I seem proud or indifferent?

Did I use humor or wit?

Was I flamboyant or very restrained in my delivery?

VOICE AND ARTICULATION

Was my speech fluent or choppy?

Did I speak loudly or softly?

Did my speech have any rhythmic quality to it?

Was I dynamic or restrained?

BODILY POSTURE AND ACTION

How much did I move?

How much did I gesture?

How much eye contact did I use?

LANGUAGE

Was my language flowery or plain?

Was I very descriptive or very concise? If I was descriptive, were the words direct and explicit or indirect and implicit?

Was my language aggressive or deferential?

CONTENT

Did I use many examples or very few?

Did I use many or very few facts?

Did I follow principles of Western logic?

Did I talk about myself in my speech?

Was I aggressively persuasive or accommodating to my audience?

ORGANIZATION

Was my logic linear or nonlinear?

OTHER OBSERVATIONS:

Speaker Observation

CHAPTER 11: ASSESSMENT

Objectives

- To increase your awareness of cultural influences on public-speaking delivery.

- To strengthen your ability to analyze the effects of different speaking styles on different audiences.

Steps

1. Observe a speaker outside class. Select a speaker and setting unlike those to which they are most accustomed. Identify a speaker culturally different from yourself, and a setting that is unfamiliar to you. You could try, for instance, attending a service of a different religion, or a meeting of a group whose members are culturally different from you.

2. Seek advance permission to attend if it is not a public event. You need to observe the rules of the occasion as well. Do men and women sit separately? Should their clothing be modest? Should shoes be removed before entering?

3. Write the "Speaker Observation" paper. Read the paper assignment thoroughly before the speech, so you will know to what to pay close attention. You should take notes at the speech; you may wish to tape it, if you have permission to do so.

Speaker Observation Paper

I. Give the following information at the top of your paper:
Your name, name of speaker observed, and specific occasion
Date, time, and location of speech
Title or main purpose of speech

II. Analyze the speech according to the following six speech categories. Use the subtopic continuums to assist your writing, discussing those that apply. Where along the continuum would you place the speaker, compared to other speakers you have seen? Discuss other subtopics appropriate to what you observed.

Speaker Attitudes
Emotional to detached
Proud to indifferent
Using humor and wit to not using humor and wit
Personal flair and flamboyance to restrained formal style

Voice and Articulation
Fluent to choppy
Loud to soft
Rhythmic to nonrhythmic
Dynamic to restrained

Bodily Postures and Action
Broad movement to limited movement
Many gestures to few gestures
Much eye contact to limited eye contact

Language
Flowery to unadorned language
Highly verbal to concise language
Aggressive to deferential language
Rhythmic to nonrhythmic language
Descriptions that are direct and explicit to descriptions that are indirect and implicit

Content
Many examples and stories to few examples and stories
Many facts to few facts
Much use of Western logic to limited use of Western logic
Objective description of the topic to subjective description of the topic
Talking about self to not talking about self
Aggressively persuasive to accommodating

Organization
Linear to nonlinear organization

Public Affairs Programming/C-SPAN

CHAPTER 11: ASSESSMENT

Objectives

- To provide opportunities for analysis of public speaking events.

- To become aware of the current and vital issues of the day.

- To provide opportunities to view diverse speakers on topics of diversity.

Steps

1. Watch an excerpt of a public speech on C-SPAN, another community-based public affairs program, or sample provided by your instructor. You may need to locate your community cable operator for the C-SPAN, C-SPAN 2, or other public affairs programming in your area.

2. Upon completion of your viewing be prepared to comment on the following:

   a. What position does the speaker hold? What is the thesis statement?

   b. Is it obvious that certain political beliefs are present? How do they appear obvious to you?

   c. Define the audience for which this speech is intended.

   d. Comment on the speaker's style and delivery.

   e. Comment on the speaker's effect on you as a listener.

3. Share your comments with the rest of the class.

*INSTRUCTOR: See Exercise Notes for this exercise in the back of the book.

Instructor Notes

INTRODUCTION

We began the project of creating multicultural exercises for introductory speech communication classes because we felt the intercultural dimensions of communication are too important to be left as elective study. As faculty, we know how tough it is to find the time to learn about multiculturalism and then find time to implement it into our classes. That is why we wrote this book. Our original product was designed for use by the speech communication faculty of our college; it has been edited and expanded to create speech communication activity manuals in a variety of communication areas.

More than most disciplines, speech communication is a good home for the teaching of multicultural issues. The speech communication classroom is a place where the need to know and to adapt to one's listeners makes understanding multicultural perspectives essential. Awareness of self as a communicator naturally should include the ways in which one is similar to and different from classmates in values, attitudes, and verbal and nonverbal communication approaches, including ideas of when to speak and to whom.

Consequently, we argue for inclusion of multicultural perspectives throughout the course, not as an add-on. We strongly believe that the speech communication classroom can provide the safe haven students need in order to address the vital yet intimidating topics of race, ethnicity, class, gender, sexual orientation, disabilities, etc., in our society.

Rather than avoid such topics or face them only in tense moments that flare, then disappear, the instructor can establish a multicultural dimension that makes cultural issues integral to the course.

To do so effectively, two parameters are essential. One is the establishment of ground rules that lead to reducing personal fears and providing a supportive, respectful, and comfortable climate for those who have pain, anger, or strongly held views to express. The class should participate in the first week in the establishment of ground rules by which all agree to abide. They might include the following:

1. No dumping or blaming.
2. Respect others' rights to their views.
3. Be open to listening.
4. There is no hierarchy of pain; it is counterproductive to weigh who has suffered most.

It is also essential that the instructor be an effective model of the acceptance and respect we ask from the students. Entering into multicultural issues creates some level of fear in the instructor as well. The instructor must be willing to say, "I don't know," and "I never thought of it that way," giving up ownership of classroom expertise in ways that demonstrate genuine curiosity, openness, and respect for all views. We cannot encourage openness and then shut it down when it gets too close to home. We need to self-explore and to be aware of our own "hot buttons." We are entitled to express our views too, but we need to demonstrate acceptance of alternatives.

A wonderful advantage of a classroom situation is that we can postpone discussion until reading and contemplation of that reading have taken place. *If an opinion expressed seems unfounded, the class can accept the challenge to find the facts to test the opinion.*

Our own experiences tell us that the more often difficult issues of cultural experience are raised, the more the instructor's comfort level grows. Simultaneously, more unengaged students become engaged, finding that their perspectives are vital to class learning. Adrienne Rich has asked, "What happens when someone with the authority of a teacher describes our society, and you are not in it?" (Takaki, p. 16). At its core, good multicultural teaching is good teaching.

What constitutes this "good teaching" in a multicultural classroom? Good teaching is part philosophy, part methodology.

Through multicultural activities, we are asking students to bring personal information into the classroom. Faculty need to be highly sensitive to protecting the egos of all students who share their perspectives in class, as well as to protecting the right of students *not* to share.

Recognizing that students have differing abilities and personalities, the use of a variety of teaching techniques is recommended. Some students may be introverted, so they can be encouraged to participate through the use of writing activities geared to helping them organize their thoughts before speaking.

There are many excellent group techniques that help students participate and think critically. (See William H. Bergquist and Steven R. Phillips, in *Classroom Communication*, for an excellent review of thirteen communication structures to involve students, ranging from a panel discussion to debates and role playing.) Some students need to be actively engaged in their learning. Group activities encourage this.

In lecture-discussion classroom situations we need to allow students time to think, to interpret their experiences in light of questions asked by the teacher, and to complete thoughts. By increasing the amount of "wait time" to three seconds or more we can increase the variety and the number of student responses. The quality of the answers should improve as well.

Students have different learning styles and the traditional lecture method may not be as effective in reaching students who prefer to learn through visual or kinesthetic channels. Techniques such as the use of media, collaborative exercises, and field trips are recommended.

The type of questions asked by the teacher is also important. If the questions are only to test the recall/memory of the students, we are not sharpening their critical thinking skills. More questions should ask students to interpret, apply, analyze, synthesize, or evaluate information and ideas. (A hierarchy of the levels of questioning has been developed by Allan Bloom.)

None of these ideas are new, but in the multicultural classroom we need to encourage students to contribute to their own learning.

Finally, we feel it is essential that multicultural study be more than appreciating differences across cultures. That is a vital step, but not a final step. If we end a course feeling separated into multiple groups, we hardly improve the level of communication in our society.

The instructor needs to guide students toward an ending-point perspective that values communication across cultures as an avenue to staying connected with fellow human beings. We have found students in despair when they have stopped at the stage in which differences seem to make connection impossible. Out of hard work to understand and respect differences grow appreciation and a sense of personal connectedness. We have created exercises in which students will demonstrate common feelings of isolation, of pain, and of feeling accomplished, effective and empowered to succeed in communication.

Using These Materials

The goals of these materials are twofold: to broaden the content of the classes to reflect the diverse cultural backgrounds of our students and our society, and to foster the use of diverse teaching practices that fit a variety of learning styles and student experiences.

Each activity is self-contained. Each one can be used in a variety of ways to stimulate discussion, set up activity/role play, provide information on multicultural issues, or offer thoughtful topics for student speaking or writing.

Each activity is designed to be as simple and as adaptable as possible. Develop them further to fit your own class needs. Time is sometimes at a premium, but it is important to allow adequate time for the class to process, draw conclusions, and resolve conflicts that develop from activities used.

Most of the activities depend on some knowledge of the concepts being demonstrated. It is essential that students be urged to read relevant class readings prior to doing the exercises. Once the expectation is built for in-class activity dependent upon reading, motivation to read chapters should increase.

We have included a section of activities in the Assessment section of this book. They range from self-evaluations to outside-of-class observations of others. Modify these assignments to meet your own classroom assessment needs and fit them in where you feel they are most appropriate.

Marlene C. Cohen
Susan L. Richardson
Tony D. Hawkins

Exercise Notes

ACHIEVING SUCCESS IN PUBLIC SPEAKING CLASS

Chapter 1: Introductory Activities

EVALUATION

Make sure you explain to the students those rules that you think are especially helpful for students in *your* class to succeed.

Have the students put in writing to you what they are willing to do to succeed in your class and have them tell you what you could do to help them achieve their goals. These papers can be read privately. You may choose to respond personally to each student's list.

COMMENTS

This exercise helps establish students' attitudes because students tend to be very honest. This exercise is useful for planning your approaches to potential student difficulties.

Not all students know how to be successful in school; this exercise familiarizes students with college culture. It also establishes an early instructor interest in student success, and helps build rapport.

EAST-WEST ASSUMPTIONS

Chapter 1: Introductory Activities

EVALUATION

Consider using the table to discuss United States values and assumptions with the whole class. You could also discuss how these assumptions influence intra-United States, as well as international, cultural conflict situations.

COMMENTS

This exercise can be done alone, in dyads, in small groups, or as a whole class. If your students are not culturally diverse in ways that would provide such East-West experiences, locate current events stories to use as examples.

Example One:
Following the death of Kim Il Sung in 1994, the changeover in leadership in North Korea was handled in a very vague and secretive manner, by Western standards. Americans may have expected a strong emergence of son Kim Jong Il, but for weeks he did not speak publicly, even at his father's funeral, and no statement was made naming the new leader. Americans may have expected an immediate, clear and distinct announcement of the changeover in power; Lyndon

Baines Johnson was dramatically sworn in on an airplane immediately following the death of John F. Kennedy, with Americans watching on television. But weeks passed in North Korea without any public statements about new leadership. Progress toward the future was not the focus of attention; Koreans were mourning.

Assumptions and values that apply to this situation are as follows:

> Thinking leads to clear and distinct ideas in Western cultures, compared to the way things emerge holistically and without precise explanation in Eastern cultures.

> Time moves from past to future in Western perspective. Thus moving on is greatly valued in our culture when a president dies. Eastern cultural values can allow for a time for mourning without a preestablished ending time.

> Communication is direct in the United States, whereas silence regarding the name of the new leader was acceptable in Korea.

Example Two:
Many Americans perceived the Singapore government's caning in 1994 of American Michael Fay as a violation of personal rights. But Singaporeans place group standards above personal rights. The more the United States protested, the more it was essential to Singapore not to show an American boy receiving treatment any different from others.'

Assumptions and values that apply to this situation are as follows:

> Individual needs may come before group needs in Western cultures, whereas in Eastern cultures group conformity often is perceived as necessary for unity.

> In Eastern cultures, punishments such as caning seem appropriate to deter crime; in the West they are perceived as violations of individual rights.

AUDIENCE SURVEY

Chapter 2: Audience Analysis

EVALUATION

After the students have selected their topics for their persuasive speech assignment, have them create their own survey for that specific topic. Discuss with the students the types of questions they might wish to ask, depending on their topics. You might require a specific number of questions (10–15) and require that they use a variety of question types. These questions might follow some organizational plan.

Have the students bring to class enough copies of their survey to hand out to everyone (including the instructor). Use one class period to have the students distribute their surveys; have the class fill out the surveys and return them.

Have the students tabulate their results as homework for the speech.

Ask students to write two paragraphs indicating what they learned from the class survey that will help them organize and present their persuasive speeches. They should answer these questions:

a. What did you learn about this particular audience?
b. How will you adapt to this audience in your speech?

You might require students to include some of the data from the survey in their speeches.

COMMENTS

Students enjoy creating the questions and analyzing their survey results. It helps them in thinking through how to approach their own speeches and links their success more closely with their audience surveys.

ETHICS

Chapter 5: Credibility and Ethics

COMMENTS

Students are likely to discover cultural differences in deciding what is ethical behavior. What constitutes cheating, lying, and taking credit for completed work (a group versus an individual getting the credit) differs among cultural groups.

This exercise also gives the instructor a chance to clarify what he or she expects as appropriate classroom behavior.

INTEREST LETTERS

Chapter 6: Emotional Appeal

STEPS

Select an interest letter that deals with a relevant contemporary issue: i.e., a letter from the World Wildlife Fund, Mothers Against Drunk Driving, or the National Gay and Lesbian Task Force, and distribute copies to all students.

Have the students read the letter and circle the persuasive appeals that are present. Begin with any visible appeals (color pictures, handwritten notes, cute logos, etc.); go through the letter with the class and discuss any attention-getting devices, needs, benefits/concerns, themes, and actions.

After they have completed the evaluation of the letter, ask the students the following discussion questions:

What was the impact of the letter on you, the reader?
How does the writer establish credibility with you?

What reasoning devices are used to attempt to get you to act?
As a result of what the writer included in the letter, what power do you have as the mediator of change?
What action of yours will have the most impact on the situation described in the letter?

EVALUATION

Ask the students for possible topic areas for the persuasive speech. Ask them to determine how they will establish their credibility with the audience, what warrants/data/claims will be used, and the potential emotional appeals.

COMMENTS

This exercise provides a clear demonstration of persuasive appeals and introduces the importance of the classroom as a forum for demonstrating effective public speaking techniques.

PUBLIC AFFAIRS PROGRAMMING/C-SPAN

Chapter 11: Assessment

COMMENTS

You may gather numerous examples on videotape of speech structure, style, and delivery. Taped C-SPAN events are within the public domain and used for classroom purposes, thus are not subject to copyright laws.

Or you may purchase C-SPAN compilation videos from the Public Affairs Video Archives at Purdue University. They may also help you search for speeches according to subject, affiliations, events, or dates. Contact: Purdue University, Public Affairs Video Archives, West Lafayette, IN 47907-1000.

Annotated Bibliography of Selected Multicultural Materials for Use in the Speech Communication Classroom

Banks, J.A., and Cherry McGee Banks, eds. *Multicultural Education: Issues and Perspectives*. Needham Heights, MA: Simon & Schuster, 1989.

> This book provides a useful and complete definition of multicultural education as well as a useful analysis of its value with relation to the special needs of ethnic minorities, language diversity, disabled students, and gifted students. It includes descriptions of four levels at which a syllabus can be redesigned to integrate ethnic content.

Gudykunst, William B. *Bridging Differences: Effective Intergroup Communication*. 2nd ed. Thousand Oaks, CA: Sage Publications Inc., 1994.

> This text is a valuable melding of interpersonal and intercultural communication concepts at an introductory level. Gudykunst provides clear definitions and examples as well as interesting self-assessment instruments.

Kaplan, Robert. "Cultural Thought Patterns in Inter-cultural Education." In *Toward Multiculturalism: Readings in Multicultural Education*. Ed. J. S. Wurzel. Yarmouth, ME: Intercultural Press, Inc., 1989.

> Kaplan looks at a composition class with students of different ethnic affiliations. He provides an important description of various methods they use to organize information. Examples demonstrate where the cultural variations are in conflict with what is expected in a standard English course. His examples illustrate the necessity for instructors to recognize cultural thinking differences when evaluating student writing, speeches, and other classroom activities.

Samovar, Larry A., and Richard E. Porter, eds. *Intercultural Communication: A Reader*. 8th ed. Belmont, CA: Wadsworth Publishing Company, 1996.

> This popular intercultural communication textbook provides a wealth of articles from the experts, organized by communication topic. Some articles explain concepts, as nonverbal types of differences, across cultural groups. Others focus on one culture or provide comparisons of two cultures. It provides a nice introduction to many intercultural issues.